A McGRAW-HILL NEW BIOLOGY

Scientific Adviser: Dr. Gwynne Vevers

SPIDERS & SCORPIONS

OTHER BOOKS IN THIS SERIES

Frogs, Toads & Newts

F. D. Ommanney
Illustrated by Deborah Fulford

A McGRAW-HILL NEW BIOLOGY

J. L. Cloudsley-Thompson

Spiders and Scorpions

Illustrated by Joyce Bee

McGRAW-HILL BOOK COMPANY
New York   San Francisco

Library of Congress Cataloging in Publication Data

Cloudsley-Thompson, J. L.
  Spiders and scorpions.

  SUMMARY: Introduces the characteristics and habits
of some common spiders and scorpions in the United
States.
  1. Spiders—Juvenile literature. 2. Scorpions—
Juvenile literature. [1. Spiders. 2. Scorpions]
1. Bee, Joyce, illus. 11. Title.
QL458.4.C55   595′.44   74-9546
ISBN 0–07–011389–0 (lib. bdg.)

SPIDERS & SCORPIONS
First distribution in the United States of America
by McGraw-Hill Book Company, 1974.
Text © J. L. Cloudsley-Thompson 1973.
Illustrations © Joyce Bee 1973.
First printed in Great Britain for
The Bodley Head
by William Clowes & Sons Ltd. Beccles.
First published 1973.

Contents

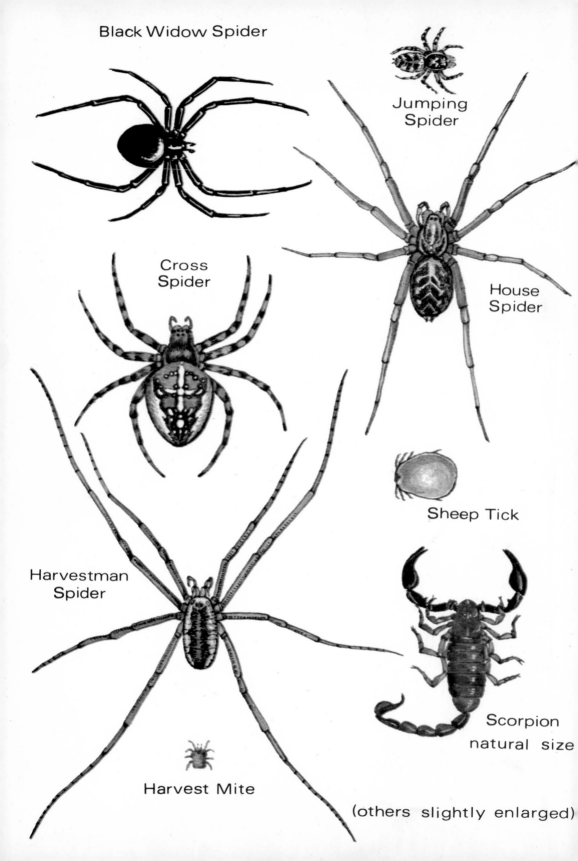

Black Widow Spider

Jumping Spider

Cross Spider

House Spider

Sheep Tick

Harvestman Spider

Scorpion natural size

Harvest Mite

(others slightly enlarged)

1
Introduction

Human beings are animals, just as goats and monkeys, birds, crocodiles, fishes, spiders, scorpions or worms are animals. But there is one important way in which we are different from the other animals. We can think and wonder; they cannot. We know that some of the things we do are good and others are bad. It is not like that with other animals. They do what they must, according to their natures.

The dog is more clever than most other animals. He learns to do what he is told. When you say, "Good dog!" he understands and is pleased. But if he runs away and you are cross with him he will be unhappy. So dogs can be taught to behave as we wish them to; but they cannot decide for themselves what is right and what is wrong.

When a dog is hungry and smells food, saliva comes into his mouth. Then he eats his dinner. The same thing happens with you and me. We do not learn to feel hungry and to produce saliva. It is automatic. Nor does a baby learn to drink his mother's milk. These things happen by instinct. When we are tired we go to sleep. That is an instinct too. Now, most of the things that animals do are instinctive. Their behavior is partly the result of learning and partly of instinct.

Warm-blooded animals which are covered with hair and feed the babies with their mothers' milk are called "mammals." We are mammals. So, too, are monkeys, dogs, cats, sheep, horses, cows, whales, elephants and mice. But we are less hairy than most other mammals.

The behavior of mammals is influenced by learning as well as by instinct. Dogs learn from other dogs as well as from people. Wild mammals learn from their parents, from other animals of the same kind, and from what they find out by themselves. Birds, too, learn from their parents; but their behavior is more instinctive than that of mammals. Instinct is even more important to animals like spiders and scorpions, which scarcely learn at all.

Just as a train must go along the railway lines, so the life of a spider or scorpion is determined from the moment it is born. Everything it does is decided in advance by the instincts that it has inherited from its parents.

In the same way, we inherit blue or brown eyes, white skin or black, fair or dark hair. We also inherit a happy temperament or a sulky disposition, a generous nature or a mean one. We cannot change our color, however hard we try, but we can learn to change our behavior. We can learn not to cry when we are hurt and we can learn to smile even when we are unhappy. Like us, scorpions and most spiders cannot change their shape or color. But, unlike us, they cannot change their behavior either.

8

2
What is a spider?

Spiders are not insects. Spiders belong to the class of animals called "arachnids." You can tell the difference quite easily. Houseflies, like all insects, have six legs and a pair of "feelers" or "antennae." Spiders have eight legs and their feeling organs are not antennae but leg-like "palps." Most adult insects have wings (not fleas or worker ants, of course)

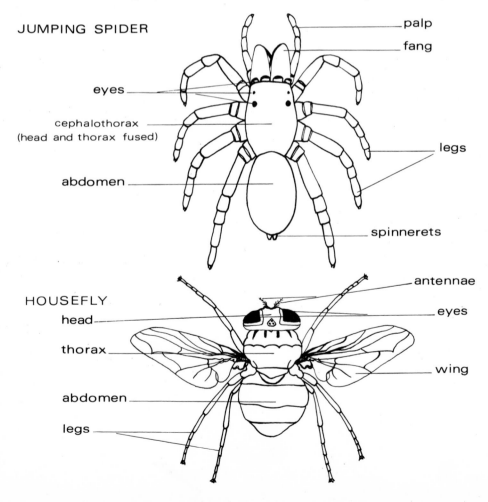

JUMPING SPIDER

palp

fang

eyes

cephalothorax
(head and thorax fused)

legs

abdomen

spinnerets

HOUSEFLY

antennae

eyes

head

thorax

wing

abdomen

legs

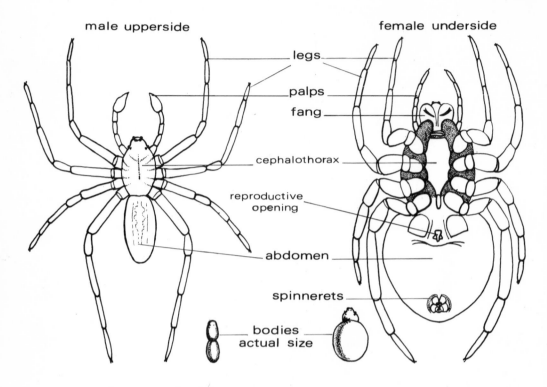

male upperside

female underside

legs

palps

fang

cephalothorax

reproductive
opening

abdomen

spinnerets

bodies
actual size

but arachnids never do. The body of an insect is divided up into three parts: the body of a spider is in two parts. Insects have two eyes, most spiders have six or eight eyes.

Spiders secrete their silk with special glands. As a sticky fluid, the silk flows down the ducts of these glands to their openings on the spinnerets. Silk leaves the spinnerets only if it is pulled. When gossamer is being produced the silk is drawn out by the wind. Before spinning its web, a spider first presses its spinnerets against a twig or leaf, and then moves away. As the liquid silk is stretched, it solidifies to form a thread.

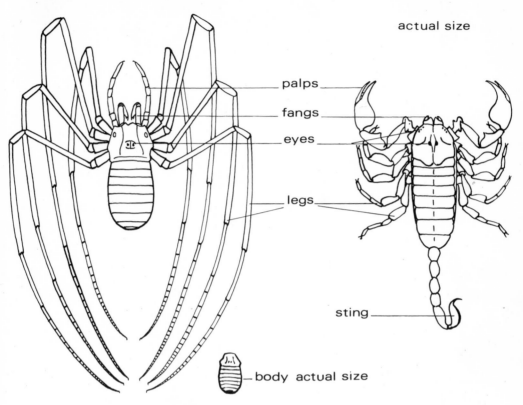

HARVESTMAN SPIDER

SCORPION

actual size

palps

fangs

eyes

legs

sting

body actual size

The animals in this book are all arachnids. Harvestmen, or "daddy-long-legs" as they are called in the U.S.A., are arachnids. So, too, are scorpions and mites, and several other animals which not many people know about. If you find a small, wingless animal with eight legs and a pair of feelers which are short, stout and not used for walking, you may be sure that it is an arachnid.

3
The garden spider

In any garden there are dozens of different kinds of spiders. They do not all look alike and they do not all behave in the same way. But the kind which we call the garden spider, or cross spider, always looks the same. It spins an orb-web with which to catch its prey. This web contains sticky threads. An insect that flies into the web of a garden spider gets stuck. Then the spider kills and eats it.

The webs of garden spiders are all the same. They have almost exactly the same pattern. The first web that a baby spiderling spins will look very much like the last one that it makes before it dies of old age—except that the first web is smaller. The spider does not need to learn how to make its web; it just spins instinctively. There is nothing clever about it. The first web is as perfect as the last one, and the spider cannot help making them all the same.

Web-building is a good example of an instinctive action. Every kind of web-spinning spider uses a different design. You can tell just by looking at the pattern what kind of spider has built a particular web. Spiders are just like little machines. Ordinarily, they cannot change the kind of web they build.

Orb-web covered with hoar frost.

Animals have two main jobs in life. The first is
to find food and keep themselves alive without get-
ting eaten by some other animal. The second is to
have babies. After the first animals have died, the
babies take their place. When these babies grow up,
they, too, have babies of their own to take their place
in the world, and so on.

"Black widow" spider (*Latrodectus mactans*) spinning her tangled web. Unlike the garden spider, she does not spin a patterned web.

4
How the garden spider catches its food

The garden spider spins an orb-web to catch its food. It does this by instinct. The web is stretched inside an irregular silken frame which is joined to the center by a large number of threads, like the spokes of a wheel. The strands of silk which make up the frame and the spokes themselves are strong so that the spider can run across them. The spokes are joined together by much finer threads that look like a series of rings. Actually these form a continuous spiral, like the spring of a clock. The spiral line is sticky. It is covered with thousands of little beads of gum, too small to see without a microscope. These little beads of gum stick to any insect that flies by mistake into the web.

From the hub of the wheel, a rather stout thread leads to a nest of leaves, spun together. Here the spider lives when it is not resting on its web. The struggles of an insect which has been trapped in the web cause vibrations of the stout thread. The spider can feel this with its legs. Then the spider runs out and bites the insect. The jaws of the spider inject a poison which kills the prey. All spiders are poisonous but most of them are too small for their jaws to pierce the human skin. And very few of those strong enough to bite us do any harm. Their poison is most effective against insects. The most dangerous spider is the North American "black widow" and her

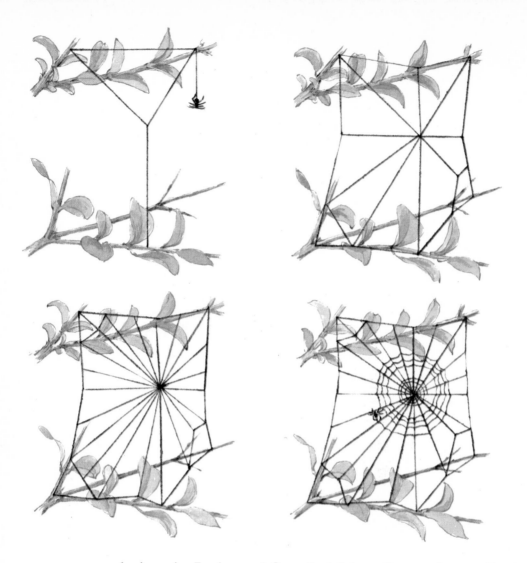

relatives in Italy and South Africa. Some Australian trap-door spiders and one or two other kinds are also harmful.

When the insect is dead, the garden spider wraps it up in silk. It stays like this until the spider is ready to eat it. If you look at the web of a garden spider you will often see a number of wrapped insects, waiting in the spider's larder to be eaten.

When a poisonous insect such as a wasp or bee

16

Stages in the spinning of an orb-web.

gets caught in the web, the garden spider does not
attack it. This might be dangerous for the spider.
Instead she cuts the web and lets the poisonous
insect escape. She does this by instinct, not because
she is clever. The struggles of a big insect cause
different vibrations from those of a small fly. The
spider's different patterns of behavior are released
by different kinds of stimulus. The spider only
attacks insects that cause rapid vibrations.

5
Breeding behavior of the garden spider

Garden spiders spend most of their lives waiting for insects to get caught in their webs. Female spiders are generally much bigger and stronger than male spiders. So it is very important that the male spider should not be mistaken for a fly when he visits a female. He does this by tapping a kind of morse code on the web. The signal that he sends in this way is quite different from the vibrations caused by a struggling insect.

Male garden spider (*Araneus diadematus*) on the right, tapping web, his enlarged palps charged with sperm. Found in America.

Before he goes courting, the male spider spins a tiny web on which he deposits a drop of sperm. This is absorbed in special bulb-like organs at the end of the palps. When mating takes place, the sperm is discharged into the opening of the reproductive organs of the female. Adult male spiders can be distinguished from females and young by the presence of a swelling on each of their palps.

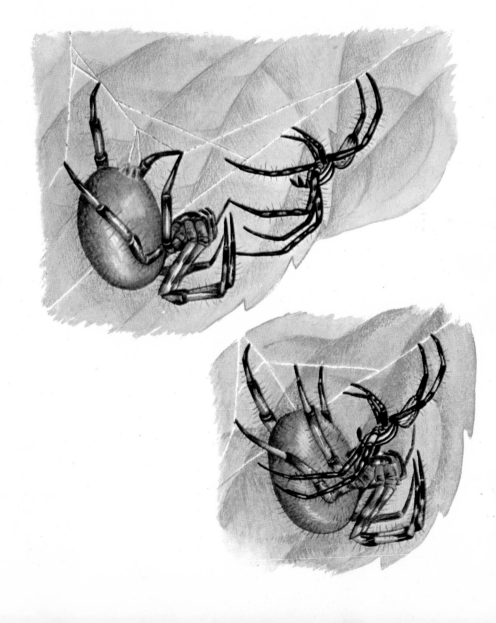

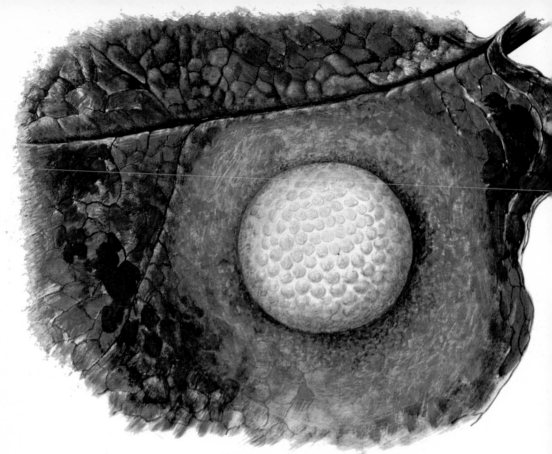

Garden spider's egg-sac with
outer covering of silk removed.

The mother spider lays her eggs on a saucer of
silk and covers them with still more silk. The silk
forms an egg-sac or cocoon, and protects the eggs.
The egg-sac of the garden spider is hidden by pieces
of vegetation so that enemies cannot see it easily.
The eggs hatch into baby spiderlings which soon
build their own webs and grow by molting.

If you open a spider's cocoon, you will see that
the eggs are very small. It is amazing that such tiny
structures should contain not only the potential of
all the complicated bodily structure, but also all the
complex instincts that will come into play during the
spider's life.

Baby spiderlings dispersing.

Funnel web.

6

Other web-building spiders

The circular snare of the garden spider is the most complicated form of spinning work that spiders perform. Cruder structures can be found everywhere. The common house spiders build funnel webs in the corners of rooms, lofts and garden sheds. They have relatives whose closely woven sheet-webs are a common sight in country bushes. These webs consist of a wide sheet, at the corner of which is a silken tube in which the spider lives. Above the sheet is an irregular mass of tangled threads. These threads are not sticky. When an insect flies into them, by mistake, it is tripped up and falls on to the sheet below. The house spider then darts from its tube and catches the insect before it can escape.

House spiders are thinner and longer than garden spiders. They can run very quickly with their long legs. One kind has a reddish band running down the center of the body. It is sometimes called the Cardinal spider because of a legend that Cardinal Wolsey was frightened when he found some of them living in Hampton Court Palace. There is no need for anyone to be frightened of most spiders. They are interesting animals and do no harm.

The male spider taps the web with his palps when he approaches the female. If she is in a receptive mood she will let him drag her to a suitable place

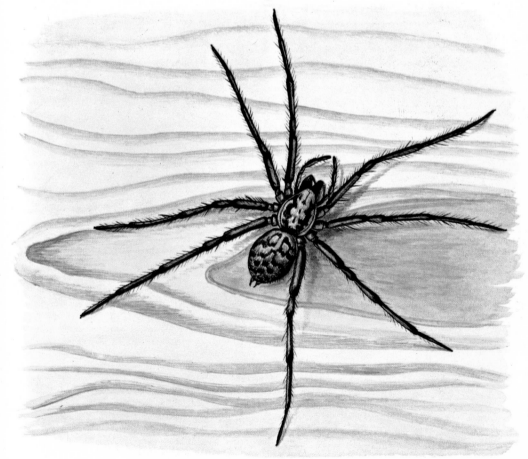

Female house spider (*Tegenaria domestica*). Female spiders do not have enlarged palps. Found in America.

on the web and mating takes place. After she has laid her eggs, the female guards the cocoon until the babies have hatched and can fend for themselves.

One of the most interesting of the web-building spiders is the water spider which lives in ponds and

Water spider (*Argyroneta aquatica*) carrying air to her home.

ditches in Europe. In order to watch it properly, you have to catch one in a net and put it in a glass jar or aquarium with a little water weed. Then you will see that, as it dives, the spider carries over its body a silvery bubble of air. This air is held by the numerous fine hairs that cover the body of the water spider. There is enough air to last the spider for an hour or more.

The water spider spins a bell-shaped web for herself under water. This is usually anchored to a water weed. The web is then filled with air in a very ingenious way. The spider grasps an extra large bubble of air with her hind legs and carries it down to her home. She does this over and over again, until the dome is completely filled with air. Here she lives, swimming out from time to time to catch freshwater insects, and even baby fishes, which she takes back and eats in her dome.

The male water spider is unusual among his kind in that he is bigger than the female. He builds a web next to that of the female and then connects the two with a tube. Afterwards he can crawl along this and mate with her.

The eggs are laid in the spring in a dense white cocoon in the upper part of the dome. They hatch within three or four weeks and the young spiders bite their way out. They may stay inside their mother's bell for another month before they molt. Finally they swim away and set up home for themselves. The aquarium is then full of dozens of glistening air bubbles, moving hither and thither as the baby spiders swim about looking for a good place to spin their webs.

7
Hunting spiders

All spiders can spin, but only some of them build webs to catch their prey. Many of them have no home: they wander about all their lives. Ground hunting spiders hide away under rocks and stones during the day. At night they come out and hunt for insects which they grab with their front legs. These are drab animals, grey, black or fawn in color. One kind lives indoors and you can sometimes find it in the evening walking across the floor or climbing on the wall.

Ground hunting spiders recognize their prey by the sense of touch. It is, therefore, not surprising that the male should court the female by stroking her front legs with his. He does this in a special way so that he is not mistaken for an insect. The eggs are protected in a thick egg-sac attached to a stone. The mother does not usually guard them.

The best known of the hunting spiders are wolf spiders, jumping spiders and crab spiders. Wolf spiders hunt their prey by sight during the day. They are very common in woods and fields. Some kinds have no home at all but wander about, spending the night under a stone or in any casual shelter. Others live permanently in holes or burrows, in the mouths of which they spend most of their time, on the lookout for passing insects. Wolf spiders chase their prey and catch it on the ground.

Jumping spiders have very large eyes and excellent sight. They stalk flies like a cat stalking a mouse. When they get close enough, they make a sudden jump, grabbing the prey with their legs. Then they give it a poisonous bite. The jumping spider of America, commonly seen on our walls and houses, is a well-known example. As they walk along, jump-

Female ground hunting spider (*Dysdera crocata*), found often under stones. This species has only six eyes. Found in America.

ing spiders trail behind them a thin line of silk. This they fasten down at frequent intervals so that it acts as a life line and prevents them from falling to the ground if they should slip while they are out hunting.

Jumping spider (*Salticus scenicus*) with its life line of silk. The palps are hidden below its big front eyes. They are common in America.

Female wolf spider (*Pardosa amentata*) with cocoon full of eggs (see p. 31). About 50 species of *Pardosa* occur in the United States.

Crab spiders have short, squat bodies and run sideways like shorecrabs do. They usually hide in flowers and vegetation where they cannot easily be seen. When an insect visits the flower to suck nectar, the hidden crab spider grabs it and has a meal. Some crab spiders can change color to match exactly the color of the flower on which they are resting. This makes it very difficult to see them.

Because wolf spiders and jumping spiders hunt their prey by sight, the courtship behavior of the

29

Female crab spider (*Misumena vatia*) on gorse. Her eight eyes
are arranged in two rows. Common in America.

male consists of a visual display. He may jump up and down, or from side to side, waving his legs and palps at the female. This curious dance is necessary to show the female that she is looking at a male of her own kind and not at a fly that she can eat. Each species has a particular dance which protects it from females of its own kind. In one species, the male catches an insect, wraps it in silk and presents it to the female as a preliminary to mating. Crab spiders also have curious mating habits. In some species, the male ties his wife to the ground with silk threads so that she cannot eat him!

When the female wolf spider has laid her eggs, she carries the cocoon around with her, attached to her spinnerets. (These are little projections at the back of the body from which she weaves her silk.) From time to time she takes the cocoon out into the sun to warm the eggs. This helps them to hatch quickly. Although the wolf spider looks after her egg-sac so carefully, her behavior is completely in-stinctive. If we removed the egg-sac and gave her a pellet of paper or a small empty snail shell, she would carry this around with equal determination.

When the wolf spiders' eggs hatch, the babies climb onto their mother's back. Here they cluster safely until they have molted. Then they scatter and live by themselves. Jumping spiders and crab spiders do not carry their egg-sacs around, nor do the young ride on the backs of their mothers. Many varieties of wolf spiders live in America. They are often found running in forests and fields.

8
The enemies of spiders

The lives of spiders are fraught with danger. The eggs are sometimes attacked by ichneumon wasps. These are parasitic insects that lay their own eggs inside those of a spider. The ichneumon egg hatches into a grub which lives inside the egg of the spider and slowly consumes it. When the time comes for the eggs of the spider to hatch, out come ichneumon wasps instead of spiderlings.

The baby spiders that do manage to hatch safely still have to face many dangers. While they are growing, they must molt eight or nine times. This is a risky process. Feeding ceases for some time beforehand, and the animal becomes inert and apparently lifeless. Presently its integument (or outer covering) splits. Out struggles the spider, pale and soft, leaving behind not only its old integument, but also the lining of much of its digestive system and breathing tubes. Sometimes, however, it fails to extricate itself and consequently dies.

Molting may be dangerous, but it is nothing compared with the terrible enemies that attack spiders. Many spiders get eaten by birds, lizards and frogs. More are killed by certain ichneumon wasps which lay their eggs on the backs of young and adult spiders. These eggs hatch into grubs. The grubs hang on and feed on the living spiders until they have killed them.

Spider with ichneumon grub living on its abdomen.

Social wasps sometimes sting spiders to death and cut them up to feed their grubs. That is bad enough, but at least it is a quick death. Solitary digger wasps, on the other hand, do not kill their spider prey outright. They paralyze the spider with a sting, place it in a cell and lay an egg on it. Then they seal up the cell and fly away. The wasp's egg hatches into a grub. This gradually devours the spider, which cannot even move, let alone escape. The behavior of digger wasps is, of course, completely instinctive like that of spiders.

Spiders are cannibals. At all stages of their life history they are likely to be eaten by spiders bigger than themselves. Other causes of death are drought, starvation, disease and infection by molds. Of the many eggs laid by every mother spider, only one or two will normally survive to hatch, grow up and have babies of their own.

9
Harvestmen

The body of a harvestman or "daddy-long-legs" does not have a thin waist like the body of a spider. The two parts into which the animal is divided are joined across their whole width. The legs are long and spindly and the eyes are on the sides of a turret, near the center of the front of the body. Another way by which you can tell the difference between a harvestman and a true spider is that the body of the harvestman is divided into segments. It is covered by small plates, like tiles. The surface of a spider's body is usually quite smooth and unsegmented.

At the sides of the eye-turrets, near the second pair of legs, are the tiny openings of a pair of glands. In some harvestmen these glands can be seen through the covering of the body and look like an extra pair of eyes. The glands produce a liquid which has to us only a faint nutty smell, but which is very unpleasant to spiders. If a spider bites a

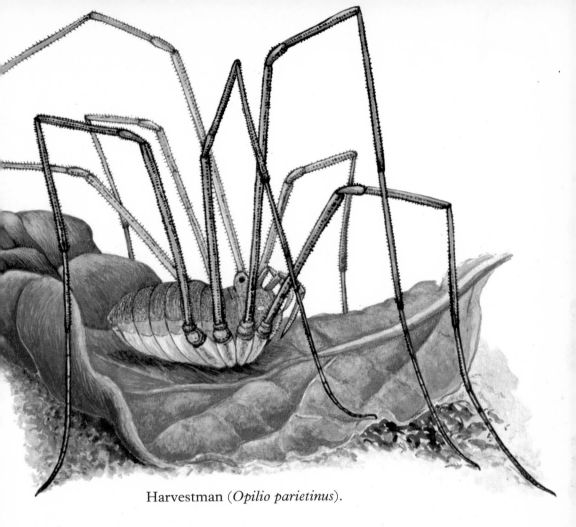

Harvestman (*Opilio parietinus*).

harvestman it will usually go away and wipe its mouth on a leaf. Very few spiders will eat harvestmen, but they are eaten by birds, frogs, toads, lizards, shrews, badgers, centipedes and various insects.

A harvestman that has been caught may sometimes escape by dropping a leg which continues to move after it has been detached. This attracts the attention of the enemy while the harvestman runs away. Whereas spiders sometimes escape by "shamming dead," harvestmen do not often do this.

Mating is a very casual affair in harvestmen. There is none of the elaborate courtship that true spiders go in for. Males and females meet each other for a brief moment and then separate. A short time later, they mate again with one another or with different harvestmen.

The females deposit their eggs, in clumps of thirty or more, in damp earth. The eggs are laid in late summer and hatch the following spring. The babies grow up by molting, like spiderlings do.

Harvestmen are usually active at night. They hide away during the day under bark, logs, rocks and fallen leaves. Their food is varied and consists of many small creatures dead and alive. If you keep them in a cage, harvestmen will also eat bread and butter, meat and fat. They are thirsty creatures and need to drink frequently.

The eggs are laid through the ovipositor, a tube which is pushed out of the female's body.

10
Scorpions

Scorpions, like spiders, are arachnids, but they are only found in warm countries. Their palps are not feelers, but big claws with which they catch their prey. They have long, thin tails ending in a poisonous sting.

Very few scorpions are dangerous enough to kill anybody, but their stings can be extremely painful. Some people think that the big black scorpions are most dangerous. This is not true. The most dangerous species are a few pale yellow desert scorpions with slender claws. It is also not true that, if you surround a scorpion with a ring of fire, it will sting itself to death.

Scorpions live in hot and tropical countries. They become sluggish in cold weather. During the day they hide away under rocks, fallen trees, down holes in the ground and in similar places. At night they come out to catch their prey. Before the sun rises, they go back to their shelter. That is why, if you live in the tropics, it may be wise to look in your shoes before you put them on in the morning. A scorpion may have hidden in one. But this occurs only very seldom. It has never happened to me, although I have lived for many years in scorpion country.

The food of scorpions consists of grasshoppers, beetles, crickets, mantids, cockroaches, moths and other insects, as well as spiders, harvestmen and

other scorpions. The prey is caught by the scorpion's claws and, if it struggles, is stung before the
scorpion eats it.

Female tropical scorpion (*Palamnaeus fulvipes*).
Her swollen abdomen shows that she is pregnant.

One of the most interesting things about scorpions is their curious mating behavior. Courtship takes the form of a dance. On finding a female, the male scorpion grasps her claws in his, as though holding hands. Then he walks forwards, sideways or backwards, while she dances with him. All the time he is feeling the ground with tiny, comb-like sense organs attached to the underside of his body.

When he finds a suitably firm surface, such as a stone, the male scorpion deposits a "spermatophore." This is a little bag of sperms on the end of a fine stalk. Then he jerks the female violently, drawing her over the spermatophore and half lifting her at the same time. She lowers herself over it and the bag of sperms enters her body.

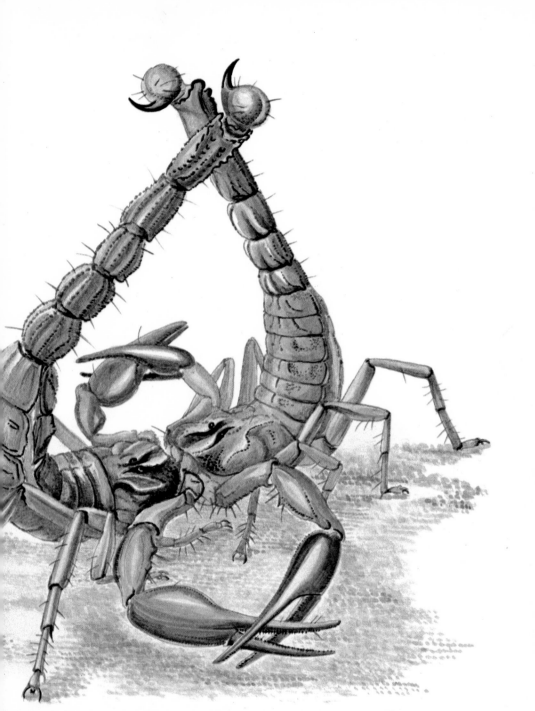

Courtship dance of *Buthus occitanus*, a scorpion found in France and North Africa. The dance will end when the male (right) feels the stone beneath him.

The fertilized eggs develop inside the mother and the young scorpions are born alive, often during the night. The babies are very plump and weak. Nevertheless, they climb onto their mother's back and remain there for a few days until after their first molt. They are soft and white. Their claws are covered with a special pad which enables them to cling to their mother's slippery back.

After they have molted, although still very small, the babies begin to look like proper scorpions. Their color is darker and they are no longer fat. Their feet have claws and they cannot ride any more on the back of their mother. A day or so later, they scatter and begin to live on their own.

Female scorpion (*Centruroides gracilis*) carrying young.
Found in Southeastern United States.

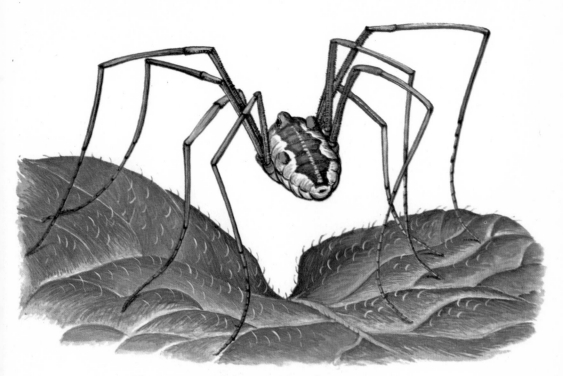

Harvestman with parasitic mites.

11
Conclusion

Sometimes you may find a harvestman with a little red ball, about the size of a pinhead, stuck to its back. This ball is a mite which is sucking the harvestman's blood. Mites are arachnids. Some of them, known as ticks, are quite large and suck the blood of mammals. There are several other kinds of arachnids that I have not mentioned. Some are very small,

others are rare, difficult to find, or little known because they only dwell in the tropics.

Scorpions are familiar, chiefly because they can sting and people are frightened of them. Some people are even frightened of spiders. Perhaps their fear is due to ignorance and the fact that spiders can run remarkably quickly for their size. No one is afraid of a tortoise or a snail.

This book is about arachnids. Compared with

Gossamer.

insects, arachnids are not very important to man. Except for mites, they do not carry disease, nor are they the pests of agricultural crops. Spiders may be useful to us, however, because they eat a great many harmful insects. It has been calculated that there are as many as 2,250,000 spiders to every acre of English countryside. These, of course, are mostly tiny black dwarf spiders that live in grass. If these spiders could all combine to spin a single thread of silk they would, in one day's spinning, produce a strand that would just about encircle the world at the equator. After ten days it would be long enough to reach the moon! The weight of insects destroyed each year by spiders in England and Wales is greater than the total weight of the human population of the country.

All animals are interesting, some more so than others. To many people, spiders and scorpions are especially interesting. I have tried in this book to explain what they are really like and how they behave.

Crab spider (*Thomisus onustus*)
on heather. Many similar species occur in America.

Index